Beautiful Soul

A POETRY BOOK ABOUT RESILIENCE

RAVYN DEVEAUX

authorHOUSE

AuthorHouse™
1663 Liberty Drive
Bloomington, IN 47403
www.authorhouse.com
Phone: 833-262-8899

Published by AuthorHouse 06/16/2021

ISBN: 978-1-6655-2724-8 (sc)
ISBN: 978-1-6655-2725-5 (e)

Library of Congress Control Number: 2021910637

Ravyn Deveaux

Ravyn was born and raised in Nassau, Bahamas. She is the last child in a large and happy family with her mother, father, three sisters and two brothers. She faced tremendous tragedy at 8 years old when as a result of Steven Johnson Syndrome, Ravyn lost 60 percent of her skin, found herself in the Intensive Care Unit of a hospital for 6 months and subsequently lost her sight after which she was never the same. She faced major challenges and suffered the loss of her mother whilst she was in the recovery process. Growing up, she did not know how to deal with her pain, her struggles, and hurt, so she started to write. She recognized that as a visually impaired poet, her story was unique and she wanted to inspire and teach others that when life throws you challenges, don't give up because you can overcome them. Thus, she wrote the book, Beautiful Soul.

What is Self-Love

Self-love is the greatest gift you can give yourself
Having self-love, you can succeed at
anything you put your mind to
I believe if you don't have any self-love you're angry with yourself
You might feel lonely with no love but let me
tell you amazing people something
If you are angry with yourself people will be angry with you
If you don't appreciate yourself no one will do it for you
Most importantly if you don't love yourself people
won't love you like you would love you
Having self-love is the greatest love

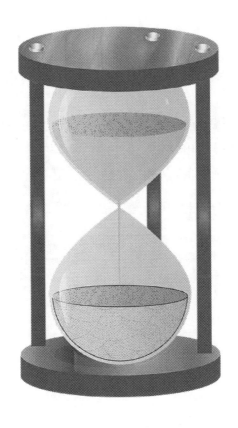

Hour Glass

Growing up was like a bird held in captivity

It felt like my hour glass was shattered

I believed my smile and presence were the

only things I had going for myself

Each day I would stick a band aid on top of my wounds

I sunk deeper into depression

I felt displaced, lost, and most nights I would cry myself to sleep

Everyday a new part of me would be ripped out

There was a point in time when I didn't know myself

I allowed people to damage me

I honestly saw no sunny days

I honestly felt useless

Some days I had suicidal thoughts

Being depressed was the only thing I know how to do

I pushed away all the people who loved me

I felt like I did not deserve them

On a physical level I knew that I was ugly

I allowed people and negative words to affect me

People looked at me very disgustingly

it hurt because I knew I was a useless

child so it was confirmation

Most times my happiness was out of reach

My Dear Beloved Ladies

There is a light at the end of each tunnel
Each dark tunnel has a lesson to be learned
You are a queen in your own right
You have the power to be successful in your body
Life is truly what you make out of it
I hope you never give up
I pray that you stay strong
Be the one who wants to turn into a butterfly
Success is all in your hands
Excellence is engraved in you
You have the power to be what you want to be
Be the best version of yourself
And when someone takes the wrong way, you take the highway
Set the tone, be different, follow your own path
My dear beloved ladies, be the leader and not a follower
Keep walking on the road to success and greatness

Green Grass

Life is not what you always think
Looking out from the inside
Makes you jealous
Life is built to make you stronger
It hurts and it's very painful
I hope you can learn from my experience
Don't be a loner
Be a Queen
Don't get jealous of people's things
Yourself is all you have
Your soul, heart, smile and presence
all makes you YOU
People walk into your life for a reason and season
When they show you their evil ways run boo as fast as you can
Don't try to keep them in your life when their time is over
Let them go
Smile and keep your head up
The lonely days will eventually turn into rays of sunshine
Excellence and success is in your reach
Grab it and reach for the goal

Alive

Waking up in the morning is a blessing
Being alive must mean you have a purpose to fulfill
and your time is not over to be on this earth
Smelling the fresh air every morning is a gift
Listening to the birds sing is a gift
Having two working eyes is a gift
Having two working arms is a gift
Having two working legs is a gift
Being healthy is an absolute blessing and a gift
Be grateful for the little things you have and
everything you have because one day you can
have it and the next day you can lose it all
Be very grateful for whatever you have
Remember, always be grateful for everything and everyone
Because everything and everyone has a
purpose just like me and you

Golden Bliss

It's amazing how people act towards others
They think you are blind of their evil ways
They think it's OK to walk all over you
and treat you like you're trash
They would use you, suck you dry and leave you for dead
They would manipulate you into believing that right is wrong
Because they believe that they are better than you
They would be your best friend when it's convenient for them
They would use you to get information and go spreading news
They would be your enemy when you
start standing up for what's right
They will always find something negative to say about you
You would bend your back, left, right, backward and forward
trying to help them and they still would dislike you
You cannot help anyone who doesn't want to be helped
They will try to control your life
Be aware of the people in your life and in your circle
The ones who aren't for you please let them go; it might
be very painful at first but you don't need negativity
And the ones who are for you, love them and cherish
them but most importantly love yourself
Not everyone who comes into your life is for you

Endless Love

Burning sage to get rid of my demons
I don't know what kinda spell you cast on me
Starting to feel bad
For all I know, losing my conscience is
something only I know how to do
What am I going through
Smelling your scent, I do miss you more
I strongly believe you are addicting
You're poisoning me with your love
Our relationship feels so right
Being with you never gets old
Loving you makes me whole
You make me feel like a Queen
When I feel like my back's against the wall you would cradle me
Your smile is something I long for
You drown me in your love

Elevation

You are not the death of me
You only make me stronger
Interacting with your negativity helps
me to become a wiser person
You trying to pull me down only allows me to rise higher
You are the elevation I needed to rise higher
Every time we interact I learn a new lesson
I will be forever grateful for the things
we've been through together
I will always appreciate you for helping me rise to the top
You were my stepping stone
I strongly believe that our door of being friends is closed
Strive for the better and I will always remember you
It was nice being your friend
I wish you all the best

My Waterfall Rain

My will to keep my head above water is incredible
Sometimes I want to drown myself in self guilt
Believing that I could make it
One of the things I've deeply struggled
with, going down the wrong path
I know that I've never wanted to do that.
The wonderful breeze from the waterfall allows me to succeed
It pushed me away from taking the
wrong path of self destruction
Having a sense of purpose is great
Believing in myself allowed me to keep my eyes on the prize
Allowing the shark in the water to make me a stronger person
Surviving a storm every time it comes my way puts
layers on top of my strength and my will to survive
I am working to pave my world of success and excellence
I am not stopping 'til the day I die and when
I do, I'll make sure my legacy lives on
The crystal clear water from the waterfall will keep on running

----

Drowning in Sorrow

Dear Angels
I would like to apologize for my incompetence
Never meant to hurt y'all
My beloved angels
No words can express the way I felt in the
moment when things went left
I apologize and I own up to my mistakes
If I can I would take it all back
This is me asking for nothing more than
closure in a situation, it's needed
I am turning my wrong into a right and this
is me saying I AM SORRY ANGELS
I wish you all much happiness, wealth and beauty
Farewell angels

Goodbye Old Friend

I was broken into a million pieces but now I am whole again
The old me with dark thoughts have ceased and now it's shining
I rarely looked at the bright side
Shining stars were not visible to my eye
Wandering the dark road seemed safe for me
Over and over again I sunk deeper into self-destruction
Never would I put myself through this heartbreak again
Down the road angle of positivity
Every day I work to put the old me behind
Rejoicing and believing I did more and more
Fill up my heart with love and honesty
Under the sun I begin to blossom
Life is beautiful
Loving myself is something I always do

Before I Throw my Cents in the Wishing Well

Please tell me how you feel when it comes to loving me

It's not worth me falling if we don't reciprocate the same feelings

Don't tell me you love me unless you mean it

I don't have the patience or decency to deal

with anybody who's playing with my life

Don't call me your wife unless we are standing at the altar

Be smart not dumb, be wise not foolish

Baby we have potential to sky dive together in true love

Don't tell me you're ready to commit unless you're ready for it

Don't tell me to run unless you're going to be

there at the finish line to catch me

Before I jump I need to know if you are going to catch me

Honestly, I am parachuting through the sky

Be pure and I will love you

In the Moment

Time and time again I question myself as a person
Loving myself seems to get me nowhere
The only thing I seem to do is hurt someone
I never understood why because all I do is try
Knowing the image that I'm painting is really crushing me
I strongly believe that I am the common
denominator of all of my problems
But honestly, I don't know how to change
I thought I was healing myself but all I'm doing is
making my problems worse giving up is not an option
but I'm stuck I don't know which way to turn

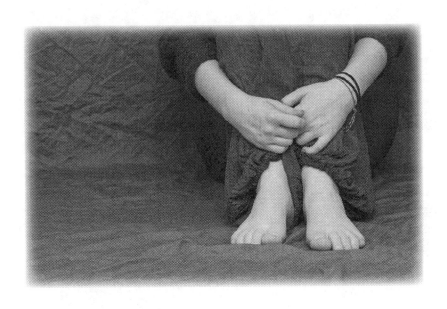

My Feelings Deep Inside

Feeling deeply broken is a feeling that I am accustomed to
Beating up my mouth is the only thing
I manage to keep consistent
Every time I take one step forward I take ten backwards
I am broken in 1 million pieces I honestly feel
like I don't deserve to be whole again
I wonder to myself, time and time again if
I really deserve people who love me
I don't want to hurt anybody I don't want to
make anybody feel bad because I am down
I don't want to drag anybody into my pain and sorrow
I honestly feel like I should be going through
it by myself and I deserve it all
I feel like all the negative things that happened to
me throughout my life is because of my fault
I believe now the best for me is the one I'm laying down
in my bed crying and chewing away at myself
And to all the people I love I'm sorry

My Journey

Being unique is something I struggled with

Developing a healthy and loving relationship with myself is hard

I work continuously trying to help myself love to blossom

The journey along the road is not easy

The pain that I endure was not bearable

The thought of giving up came frequent

Succumbing to my negative thoughts were once easy

Believing in me was incredibly difficult

I thought my pain was permanent

I know if I wanted to change my life I

had to change for the better

Printed in the United States
by Baker & Taylor Publisher Services